BRICKS AND MORTAR

Paul L Quant

ISBN 978-1-291-57103-5

Dedication

To David

Author's Note

There is a saying that walls have ears. Whether this is true or not, I maintain that walls, like waterfalls, woods and the stars, can become sites for original expressions of the imagination and this small book aims to demonstrate such a claim. Particular walls I go by presented opportunities to try different styles of poetry writing, from the precision of controlled rhyming forms to the freedom of blank verse and from the mysterious to the amusing.

The poems began to take shape as I walked around Little Downham, a village close to Ely in the Cambridgeshire fens [described by estate agents as 'sought after'] where I have lived since January 1981. I have grown to love the place, to look carefully at it and to find ways of representing it. Drawings and paintings came earlier but using walls as starting points for this small anthology was a stimulating challenge that gave me a lot of pleasure. A final thought - Why not take this book out with you, wander around the village to find the places described and maybe stand and read the poems close to the walls mentioned?

Paul L Quant

September 2013

Cowbridge

Its arched back holds the running road overhead;
Slowly underneath winds a tiny water line
While rich grasses quarrel for light and sublime
Wild flowers looked down below,
Down below.
Locals made light of its posture, had said

The old bridge just needed a straightforward name.
As cattle over its mottled stone would advance,
In indolence gaze with an undergrowth glance.
Wild flowers made sway below,
Down below,
Led by slight breezes and the swerve of the drain.

'Cowbridge' it was called but its ramparts made jest
Of the weight it supported above its tiny stream,
Cows chewing the green grass as if in a dream;
Wild flower sirens below ,
Down below,
Welcoming lovers at the bridge's broad request.

Deep down in the long grass, as if out of sight,
Stirs the softness of affection's shy interplay.
A glance up the slope lifting the past to today
Makes wild flowers sing down below,
Down below,
Unconcerned by the herd walking by to the night.

Baptist Chapel

In confidence it was created
Doors wide opened; those inclined
Went through into its understated,
Non-conformist paradigm.

Where now the dozens on a Sunday
Filing in with sober shoes
Past the preacher in the doorway
And the children? Where the clues?

All around this bleary morning
Local people otherwise
Breakfast, read the paper, yawning,
Pass time by with silent eyes.

Two, on horseback, stride down Main Street,
Halt to let a tractor pass,
Glance inside; their faces meet
The congregation through the glass.

Songs of praise from every face
Are silenced in the atmosphere
Held spinning in this hollow place.
Both look surprised but cannot hear

The past still present; harmony
In stoic pride attesting to
Past lives put by that will not be
Dismissed. The tractor passes through

And slowly go the puzzled pair,
Onwards to stables, steps away.
Hymns lifting in the locked-up air
Heard by nobody else today.

Takeaway Shop Wall

The outside wall is edged with wide,
Repeated tiles that affirm an age,
A glimmer of a golden cloud that now
Slides straight up to the roof from the path,
Turns, pauses and sets off
Along the apex of the shop.

Look through the plate glass window;
Look into the inside of this Art Deco-edged box where
Four chair backs lean against the roadside wall
Ignoring today's outdoors.
The flashing sign set on the counter
Is red like a church's sacred oil lamp,
Is less than a mirage.

This shop space has been a staging post
For babies' clothes, bread,
Anglers' knick-knacks and groceries
Though its tiled edge, brittle, unbroken,
Refuses to fall away.

Wall Outside The School

These shy bricks exude confidence,
A vision of a grand domain
Where servants moved about, a sense
Of past times in the summer's rain.

But fortunes changed and needs arose
For local space to utilise
For education; powers propose
A school with rooms of paradise.

A temporary, flat-roofed hive
Became the focal honey-pot
For parents bringing young to thrive,
To learn to live amongst a lot

Of others, rough or cherry sweet,
Some neatly clad, some very tall;
Such howls of joy and running feet,
The playground entertained them all.

 When once inside, the classes formed
A concentrated, grand advance
On maths and scientific norms,
On language, art and modern dance.

One Thursday, I remember well,
As shone the sun, no sign of rain,
They knocked it down and down it fell
And, phoenix-like, built up again.

We see renewed this precious space
With subtle lines for modern needs.
New young ones fit the present race,
A new year's worth of human seeds.

Can anyone remember when
That high and ancient barricade
Was built, or when the blackened fen
Was home at night? That mixed brigade

Pushed out the doors and left behind
Those memories that gently fail.
They surface, when the mood is kind,
See time spent in that scholar's jail.

Wall Fronting The Garage

Hardly high enough,
Too shy to interfere
With contemporary stuff,
The cars parked here;

Pristine in neat line,
Long-term won't remain;
Home's here for a time
Then gone again.

Gapped, like children's teeth,
New cars' customs post
Topped with tiny plants,
A short-term host.

Should it be removed,
Ought it disappear,
No longer loved.
Does anybody care?

Remember where it kneels,
Low, beside the street.
Cars they go on wheels,
Walls can't move their feet.

Lodge Wall

Lowly on the ridge above the green,
Testing all conditions,
Gazing down to Ely by the gently sloping road
And hardly noticed by pedestrians.
Confined, avoiding every passing pair of eyes,
Its regal garden buttressing restless lives.
Windows shade against the occasional sun,
Postal services stop there and go
And the gate latch clicks.
A solitary dog pads by, not worrying to turn
Nor stop.
Nothing seems to happen.

But I suspect its history calls out,
That such a situation longs to tell its days,
Anguishes about its settled place,
Wants to widen out some more,
See cities far away like Antioch, Rio, Singapore,
Feel deserts dreamy air, the South Seas' heat,
The hurrying streets of old New York,

The frosted Russian Steppes,
Parisian charm,
Cliffs,
Anywhere.

A car backs into the drive,
Footsteps on the gravel;
A key turns
In the lock.

Nissen Hut

In meadow-coloured camouflage by a row of evergreens
Lies an arch-roofed hut. Just begun, down streams
The pouring rain, clattering on its corrugations,
Sliding away like a comb through long hair. Conversations
Within, though shielded from the warfare going on,
Now stutter by as two farmhands stand as one,
Commenting on the day's outdoor impediment:
What can't be finished and what all this has meant
For the imminent harvest. Humidity outside
Grips the air that comes straight in on a summer's tide,
Hurries by to occupy the black interior darkness.
Their manly statuary does not move. In seriousness,
Discussions meander among common refrains,
While the cloud force determines to stay. It still rains
So in time they nod, decide upon an altered plan,
To go, go back to some other job, work indoors
For a while, as the artillery barks and the rain pours.

Shiplap By The Shop

Shiplap
Trip up,
A heap of trash,
Crumpled,
Sunlight faded wood
Unevenly constructed,
Corrupted by
The many men who
Thought they could
Make good, make cash.
Splash
From a passing dog;
Look away.
Now dead, the shop in time
Will turn into
A betting shop
I bet.

Crown Crest

The crown was lost and never found,
Though half a crown I sometimes had,
So big and silvery, thick and round;
Amazing treasure, I contend,
For piggy bank or else to spend.
(I was a rather spendthrift lad.)

The crown was lost when cruel King John
In devious ways depressed the land.
He crossed the Wash and it was gone,
Down into the rising sea
And not discovered. Even we
With modern methods close at hand

Still fail to lift that crown on high,
To watch it sparkle, jewels shine,
To claim the Kingdom as we cry
'May God protect our latest king,
Bring him the victory we sing!'
(It's just a dream – It won't be mine)

But on this wall a plaque resides;
I wonder, does it mark the place
Where, deep beneath these footings, hides
An ancient object, still asleep,
As days of our lifetime creep?
Not even half a crown, no trace.

Football Stand

Young bodies run and swerve in football games,
Disturbing shouts are mixed with grins,
Call, 'Pass!' or, 'Shoot!', echo each other's names;
A war on matted green begins.

Metallic minds compete in football games,
Intend accumulating wins.
Zigzag strike paths define the players' names;
No armour worn to cancel sins.

White chalk lines mark the bounds of football games;
The moment comes, the fight begins.
The iron castle keeps a list of names
Scratched on its corrugated limbs.

Village Centre, Village Hall

This place, this palace, belongs to us;
Our sideways glances disguise worship,
Each look a recognition not of its walls,
Its windows and its roof,
But of our very selves.

We are its space: its emptiness just a mirage,
Its inert nature nothing but a spring
For the water of our lives,
The assertion that others lived here,
That we live here, in this village, with its
Intimate buildings
Covered over by deep time,
Encouraging a network of internal, uncommon minds
To become, grow, intertwine and
Finally recede.

Meanwhile
We pass close by this shrine,
Give it a subconscious genuflexion
Which it graciously accepts.

A Post Box in a Wall

A letter, flat and folded, neatly typed,
Tucked up inside,
Stamped, stuck and posted,
The last of all
Into the red-mouthed wall box,
Now blocked,
Redundant.

Rub your hand over its rusting, cast-iron, crackled face,
Then feel the fingers of the past
That held the pulsing of words;
Wonderings,
Hopes subdued, demands,
Businesses impotent or important,
Loves, lies, confessions,
Simple words from home,
Another begging note,
A death.

Locals' stringed wordings
Held,
Collected,
Moved away and spread;
Those fettered lines in days delivered
To be read.

Blacksmith's

Rusty sheet steel door cuts away
Slides and rumbles

The light inside flicks white
Like a light bulb ill-wired

Hiss of furred acetylene flame
And then it's finished
Then a crack put-down of the face-shield

Face wipe with hand back

Regular hard file rasping
Rasping in grit-grey waves then
Dust down

Take up the iron and see the shining edge

Another job
Done

Another job to be
Done

Corrugated Iron Wall

Keep out! Keep out! No other reason comes to mind,
No logic, sentiment, no use that's subtle, accidental
Shouts or whispers; nothing slightly incidental.
In fact, I withhold all judgement,
Tell myself that I must stay content
With a blank, unreasoned kind of reason
Far in distance in my mind from treason;
Why, oh why, raise metal corrugations?
Could this be, some ask, where congregations
Gather on a deep December night,
Wrestle, box, play chess without the need for light?
Maybe local molly dancers slap about
Most brightly-clad? There are some here who doubt
Concerning these and all the other sports
Close to this dented fence; no men in shorts
Nor maidens, elegant in silken dresses,
No children slushing mud and making messes.
No, it's just a corrugated barrier, green,
As valuable as wiped-on, sun-block barrier cream.
I've had my say; not said too much unkind!

Telephone Box Wall

A box? So many different things come into mind,
For nails, screws and items utilitarian in kind;
Impressive, too, a box at the theatre for the well-to-do,
Affords superiority for those people who
Prefer to peer down on the masses occasionally.

A boxing match, for those who cuff in legal barbarity,
A van for horses moved many miles to yards,
A kind of wood so bright and hard.

O, such a useful object,
Requiring no respect.
They even put you in one
When, finally, your time has come.

Oh, I almost forgot: for public phones there's no exception.
Against intruders' ears, their protection
Now provides a minor space
For fewer of the human race.
A mobile phone, always at hand,
Supremely marches through the land.

Wall With A Gate

The gate is impotent, erect, with a 'come hither' look,
The wall down low seems normal and content;
An ordinary day, thick cloud, blustery and cold,
Not bursting over those minds that took
The road past and, like time, grew old.
I stopped to wonder what the gate now meant.

I reached and felt the gate's top hinge encrusted with disease,
The peeled white wood staring out meekly, shy,
Not wanting to make excuses for appearing dull,
Not liking to seem that it needed to please
Anyone wanting the day be full,
A lover, or simply a passer-by.

In spite of such attention I didn't join in the game
But thought of pushing through, along the path
Restricted by bushes leaning on the tunnelled air
That never moved, still trapped, always the same,
Wood spikes entangled everywhere,
A journey someone had arranged for death

To wait, then pounce. I struggled in the place I did not know,
Strained through the gap, emerged beside the road,
Rested one hand on the wall, there to feel sadly cold,
Much troubled by the past where children slow
The time when they will grow old.
I leant against the wall as my tears flowed.

Mill

The round tower sighs without a sound, its times
Remote in the eye of today's sharp designs,
Its shadow cast on fields where strawberry lines
Evidenced labourers standing.

Blackened bricks fired daily by the fen light,
Mossy scar lines fissured where the blight
Of winter is scaled crawl to the sails' height,
The sails no longer standing.

The dizzy blades spoke softly to the men below,
For centuries the cultivators, repetitious, slow
To leave behind the broken soil, to outwards go
From their sure standing.

As the bad guns called, distant at the Somme,
At Ypres, for dancing into death, then they were gone,
Did not return to droves. Its constant work was done,
No gentle landing.

Sing loudly every day, old windmill, a lament;
Sing folly, folly, to our days. Sails, rise again, intent
On turning like the sun's expected, bright consent,
Your walls still standing.

Behind The Hedge

The high hedge, like the hand of a policeman
Warns, 'Stay back, no closer please!' A man
With a long lead and a dog comes by, glances
At the hedge a moment only, takes no chances.
Confident that indifference is the best option,
He disappears with vanishing locomotion.

Across the road, a modest car waits, still, unattended,
Engine quite cold. Its late driver pretended
Not to look at the hedge across the airy gloom,
Turned aside down the short path to the Post room.
Like a main thoroughfare in a cowboy show
The theatre had emptied. The roadway opened so

The main protagonists could stand up in
The road where the gunfight would begin.
They both were bronzes, their forms the finest,
Hardened by sunlight. The sun took its highest
Point in the heavens. No onlookers got
To witness the body slump, heard the shot.

Between the hedge and the shadowed plaster,
Another body. The sun dropped faster,
The car puttered off. A trio of strangers together
On horseback filled the space. A smell of leather
For a few moments held the air.
A door slowly closed. No body was there.

Sun

Protected by, not from the sun, a house
Looks up and down the street and all around
With proud-paned windows, elegant, designed
For quietude; impressive, seemly, sound,
Assured, not like the shrinking mouse
Beneath the woodpile, burrowing underground.

Those who had lived there cared for how it looked,
Its upkeep grown from insights of good taste;
Its preciousness inevitably viewed
By locals and by strangers who, in haste,
No more than glanced but clearly hooked
Into this landmark pivotally placed.

However, in the past, when wild fires pounced,
The mercy-men, the firemen, drove their teams
When called for by some desperate messenger,
Only to veer off when a brass sun's beams
Were missing. Danger sharp-announced
By shouts, by rasping, choking nightmare screams;

Smoke sloughed the streets nearby, poured from the fire
And victims from the conflagration ran:
All saw the need for instant remedies
But nothing would amend the watering ban
Though flames wrapped up even higher.
Insurance missing, lessons there began

As nightmares for most villagers who froze,
Unable to pay dividends, secure
The use of fire prevention remedies,
Breathe comfortably in their beds, unsure
That, if flames their houses enclose,
A fire brigade would come, affect a cure.

Wealthy, the owners of that lovely home
Engaged The Sun Insurance Company;
Agreed co-operating payments would be made
To bring the pumps, the men; also agree
A golden sun on high be shown
Upon the wall – Still there for all to see.

Electricity Sub-Station

This place is contaminated by feral powers.
Its mode of operation lets it work for hours,
Days, years, decades, hemmed in by brambles, scrub and shade
Until some thunderous storm swipes with its blade,

Taking no prisoners, mercy left for other skies
To contemplate. Its hard-wired heart gives in and dies.
In consequence, no power moves in village wires,
And blackout climbs on backs, rebuffs desires.

The radios, fridge-freezers, shavers, driers, lights,
All electricity-dependant, know their rights
But cannot argue with the earthing's morbid chill,
Insistent, closing down, inhuman will.

We are unable to present a valid plea,
Persuade this dead-pan box make good, switch on, to be
Our hidden servant, catalyst, our dumb high priest,
Desist from ruining our daily feast.

The fault in time repaired by several able men,
We smile, we sigh, turn on the box, the kettle then
Forget the gift this curious power can manifest,
Sink down and soon forget this awkward guest.

Renewed Wall

The lights went out so gradually, one by one
Then quiet weeks encouraged brambles' arms.
Cracks first sighted years past had long begun
To gather pace and camouflage such charms
As once it drew.

Then fractured breath ceased totally. Rain and cold
Were bleaching agents blocking out the space.
An agent's board, bright-coloured, saying 'Sold,'
Announced the advent of its changing face.
The spring winds blew.

The builders' efforts magnified. Dusty earth
Rose. Disappearing skips sent down the street.
New window frames, set straight, began the mirth
The old place needed, ended its retreat.
The promise grew;

Completed, tidied up and furnished, giving
Newcomers kind moments, holding their space.
Now laughter from the children fills the place,
Becomes the means of always living
In morning dew.

Busy Shop Wall

A misnomer, that, for walls don't work,
They watch the shop staff people who
Are very clear they have much work to do,
Make smiling salutations, glean the news
From customers who come to buy
Tobacco, tins of peaches, just to spy
On newspapers or chocolate.

At night, before it gets too late
And needing to anticipate
New day's surprising workday ring,
Mixed customers their custom bring
While in the shop the walls of stock
Are rebuilt close beneath the clock
That evermore ignores the human games.
The sun long lost is done for, damped down flames.

Slide forward, back, deep money till;
This day concludes but soon another will
Take up the pattern, twist the key and then
The invitation sign to 'Open' once again.

Pound Wall

A dangerous electric shock
If you go over this wall and mess about
With the transformer,
But you may peep
Over the brick edge

And close your eyes then open them.
Which animals are held in there today?

Today there are just a few piglets
Snuffling in its mud.
One looks up
And sees you looking back,

Gives a singular snort
Then you are ignored.

Blink and look again.

This time three lambs
Stand huddled.
Where have they come from?
Why have they not been missed?
Do they belong in that field, over there?
Perhaps
The farmer is busy
Else why would he not understand that
They are here, missing?

A sneeze;
Look down.

The pound is full of laughing children,
Boys pulling pigtails,
Girls grouped together for security,
Hardly room to move;
Disguised cries of joy and false screams of terror.

Bit by bit I watch them grow,
Become teenagers, adults and
A silence clouds the pound as I hear a lorry
Coming closer and stopping;
Brakes on.
Tailgate dropped down
And the pound
Emptied.

Garden Fence

A sweet garden fence saw an odd occurrence;
Said a giant hedgehog, 'Won't you come for a dance
In that nearby long grass which breezes make sway?'
''That's really not likely, not really the way

For a lady-like hedgehog, so honest, so pure
And so independent, so shy, so demure,
So inclined towards silence, not socially grand.'
With these words off she scuttled, her handbag in hand.

Pacing proudly, departing, with nose held up high
She swiftly was hidden from view. With a sigh
The male of the species, his chances expired,
He rolled up and slept and forgot his desired

Lithe little hedgehog, who'd left in a fright,
Who'd slink back that evening and stay for the night.
At least, that's what he wished for, what in his heart
Remained quite distressing, made him wake with a start.

For while had had slumbered, his passions contained,
The skies they had clouded, the rain it had rained.
His prickles dripped raindrops, his chin damply soiled,
The garden awash, his hopes now all spoiled

By the weather. His lover, who'd seen this all coming
Had gone 'neath a shed, moving fast, swiftly running.
The distance between them, though yards, could be miles;
Still she sleeps, dry and warm, her face wrapped in smiles.

So, hedgehogs and others who think what they say
Will surely come true, at the close of the day,
Reflect on this story and don't be so intense -
Accept life as it comes, maybe sit on the fence.

Old Rectory Wall

We find it hard to understand the reasons
Why, those yesterdays, the Church conspired
To demonstrate that, in its seasons,
Swollen dwellings were required.

Why did incumbents have a need for power?
Why, when Christ himself spoke simple ways,
Did black-dressed clerics upwards tower,
Magnify depressing days?

They're gone below to solitude in churchyards
No more able to affect our lives:
Sleep in peace, you feeble lifeguards,
Though your rectories survive.

Should we now glorify this pile before us,
Praise the muted style of window frames,
Smile at what seems grand; our chorus
Place the past in sunset's flames?

Sturdy lines of brickwork beg another chance,
Chimneys high up incense winter's skies,
Yew hedge grows a sober, noble glance
At nothing nice, only goodbyes.

House With A Date High Up On The Side

The year in question passed away;
No action in it now remains,
No month, no week, no stubborn day,
No birth, no death, no one complains.

The present has to overcome
Past time, but what to do with the
Unwanted year that has all gone
Affected minds incredibly

'Just leave it in the history books,
Inert, describing what occurred,'
Said some. 'But what if no-one looks?'
Said others, 'That would be absurd!'

Time passed. No resolution came
Along to end this quandary
Till one (I can't recall his name)
Secured it for posterity.

A stone was inscribed with the date
And, high upon a chimney stack,
Was fixed so all might know its fate
For, as we say, 'No turning back.'

Hairdressers' Wall

Soft gossiping within the precious shop
A second purpose brings to those who crop
And wash, curl, perm and let the remnants drop,
Sweep up the snippets from the floor,
Peer through the windows primly,
Watch the day go dimly
As had the day before the day before.

Parked cars exhale the few who enter in
The fashionable premises to win
A novel outlook, ready to begin
With every confidence
A life-approach perfection;
Hair posing rich attraction,
Encompassing no limit on pretence.

The day's amount of sunlight dropping fast,
Creative hands work magic on the last
Invader entering. The shift slips past;
The hour is getting late.
Check that the room's foundations
Match up to expectations;
Tomorrow's clientele already wait.

Oldest Dwelling

It cannot hide; it crouches at The Anchor's edge,
Thatch-cropped, a freckled, pebble-dash
Leftover from history; the beaten ground beneath
More than a cradle for a floor, its windows
Eye sockets for the floods of days.

Come close up to it, sense the waves it must have heard,
The annual fling, the spring birds,
The kind of traffic of the street:
Heavy old carts, clattering echoes,
Thin children growing older,
The next easily-missed flick of
The muted stream.

Across the rutted road horse chestnut saplings
Muscle into the sky; bells at the church
Bang the hours, the funerals, the joining of hands.

It is buttressed by parked cars,
Modern homes and a shaded footpath,
Passed by lorries, baby buggies,
Mobile phones and all today's frippery.

Put your ear to the wall; a kettle boils for tea,
Draining down into this quiet old building.

Very New Wall

Though you didn't see it, now you certainly do:
Such an evenly perfect wall, so very new,
Built by a building firm, scaffold in place.
See the rows of bricks rise at incredible pace,
Whistling workers yellow-hatted in boots
With their toe-caps of steel and their workaday suits
Shuffling about with their confident glances,
Cement mixers swishing in smooth mixing dances
Then a pause at twelve-thirty for lunch in the shed
And a bit of a doze as the sun overhead
Begins its descent in the warm afternoon
But is shortly confounded by drizzle and gloom.
The wall is continued as far as the eaves
Till the rain falls much harder and wind in the trees
Calls a halt to the progress. Tools packed away
And the van doors are opened to close up the day
As quiet returns and dog walkers go by
Glancing at the new wall that approaches the sky.
Soon the house will be occupied, builders moved on,
The wall a reminder of what they had done.

Community Rooms

Push back the iron gate then slowly stride;
The clock's hands overhead not turning round,
Reminder that these walls surround
Elected space. Now step inside,

Take in the view; consider what it means
To be low down. Seep underneath the floor,
Go out of sight beneath this store,
As if below some shrunken dreams.

Look at the wall: there is a banner clear
Exhorting visitors to praise the Lord.
Good hymns once dazzled in accord,
Their memory still potent here.

A simple faith, an independent eye,
A challenge to the manor's hold
Now melted into time that's old,
That, too, is sunken, lost and dry.

Will anything shake people back to stare,
To lift hymn rhythms not to be ignored;
Bring, hand in hand, in high accord,
This way? I say, it isn't there.

And things are lost and such things stay away.
The room is dimly empty. Only folk
Who queue for stamps and share a joke
Come in, then step into the day.

St Leonard's

What happens when the candlelight is spare
Inside St Leonard's flint-knapped time-trapped face?
Do bats confide in slicing through soft prayer
That winds about its downcast, back-lit race?
Come, let's look through the window's sullen pane,
Stand tip-toe tall, eyes tightly wired and strong;
Few strings of life now link its stony frame
To outward life that hums a human song.

Around our feet the grave bricks bow and fall,
The wrinkled weed-scrub strokes each puzzled face.
Whose is the hand that built this towered wall
With instincts gripped by certainty and grace?

A lorry brakes then moves on slowly by,
A child wrapped in a buggy bundles past,
Rooks in the chestnuts shriek in candled cry;
The congregation leaves, the door made fast.

The air inside the church is stained with sound
That hollowed out its hallowed share of years.
Its snuffed light seems all sprinkled around
Its blotted boundary as it disappears.

Sheltered Archway

We die. Of that there is no opting out,
No future if we scream and shout,
Nor if we smile, nor if we pout;
That's that.

We live. At least, we might conform,
Behave at school, accept the norm,
Look bravely at each social storm,
Forgive

Or misbehave, and life rebuff,
Affirm dissent, not get enough
Of sex, appear imperious, tough,
Immune.

But later life is overblown
Yet while still breathing on our own
We need, however we have grown,
Shelter.

This opened wall accepts our past
Without a judgement, holding fast
Our hands a while, up to the last
Moment.

No gate to barricade the way,
Encouragement to stay, to stay:
A short arrangement, till the day,
That's that.

Telephone Exchange, By A Layby

An outpost of the village charged with a going
out, skis on lines, drooping and rising,
flying the fields to stream
such words we wanted
to give away, receive.

Age now tucks into its bricks
and dangles from the sky with newly-clustering hands.
Now-time drips onto the old building,
tells it it's no longer necessary, has
no further dependencies
since its adventitious roots were cut through
and satellites swung into space their novelty.

Paddock

Watching the white clouds move aside the sky,

The white horse stands
Sweeping flies away, bending down in the short grass
Meadow lands
Fenced around gently with even poles of pinewood.
Young girls' hands
Brush its back and sides, lovingly caress its neck.
Saddle-tight bands
Buckle beneath its stomach, the leather saddle securing;
The gate waves;
A holding of the reins.
The white horse is padding down the Hurst,
Pretends
Freedom is today down the uneven roadway then
Back along the track, its bends
Shallow and bitter. The gate a crack that closes,
Abandoning restraints.
Hiding very shamefully is the wooden shack
That delicately shades
One small, white, worked-out soldier.

Pond Lane House Wall

Now teasels' scratching heads are silhouettes on guard;
Wild hedges tilt towards the roadway.
He is not there; his absence drops hard
Hailstones cackling the roof in tinkling play.

The back lean-to has somehow lost its latching door;
Concealing undergrowth contrives to spread
In all directions. Can I be sure
He isn't there, that he is really dead?

Deep in the weedy waste no heavy footprints show
His stumbling paces and his brash voice.
See him, alone in one low room, go
Sit down and still the tremors of his choice.

The armies of new houses come up close and push,
Taunting this old building's failing pride;
Bold forces lean on it in a rush,
To break its dumbstruck walls, smash every side.

Trace round the sky the ways his voice, his look, his grin
Contacted days and echoed around
His homely place, lifting to a din
To show him there - Who says he can't be found?

Pub With Nautical Connections

The days outside seem empty
But empty glasses fill
From hidden metal barrels
Frenzied with sensations.

'The rain is due, like tax
That must go to the Government.
I tell you, soon there will be changes,
Up the price of beer
And petrol. Nothing stays the same,
You know. Another?
Oh yes, I've heard it all before,

How life is hard and I could scream,
I could. Do you know,
Just the other day, there was a man
In here whose coat was torn.
Slept in a field across the way, he had,
Till opening time.

Who's that, just walked by?
You didn't see them? With a big dog
And hand in hand, too.

What was I saying?
Oh, I agree with you,
Too many around here,
Not that I'm, well, bothered, but...

Another?
That's good of you.
The Market's not the same, either, Is it? Mostly rubbish, I say.
Look,
They've gone back the other way.
Time?
Quarter past – Must go.
Where's my keys? Don't go for that one,
That there big red car;

It's really not
As good as
They
Say it is.'

A Pair of Walls

There is a line,
A fine line,
A line that joins and divides,
A moment in time line,
A leap into turning the corner line,
A vertical line, bottom to top,
Where it comes to a stop,
A full stop,
That flattens out.

Below the wall there's another line
That underlines the wall,
A jagged line.

On top of this wall,
The one I have outlined,
Sits a marmalade cat.

Long, Tall Wooden Wall

That wooden wall – What might it hide?
With X-ray eyes I gaze inside.

I sense a shiny Rolls Royce car,
Red cherries in a stoneware jar,
Crates filled with bars of foreign gold
Too heavy to be ever sold
In Paraguay and jewels too,
That tiger from the Berlin Zoo,
A yacht with sails reduced to shreds,
A pair of old four-poster beds.

What's more, as someone had foretold,
A further crate of foreign gold.

Within a decorative chest,
Wrapped up, secure, five of the best
Paintings, Impressionist, not fakes,
By Renoir, and a plate of cakes.

What else? A castle, bridge and moat
With oarsmen gliding in a boat,
A cheery crowd of football fans,
A second reading of the banns
Of bride-to-be and architect,
Both twenty-three. I can detect
A frog, asleep. I still look on.

Shortly the sun sinks and is gone.
Such treasures disappeared from sight,
The fence stands guard throughout the night,
Soft footprints pad the outer path.

Not true? If I forget to laugh
Life loses that which makes it good;
I love that curious wall of wood.

Lorry Yard

Down the sloping road to West Fen
Some big sheds, big doors,
So solid where easy men
Leave lorries. These stores

Are useful for what
Might be left there,
At that indifferent plot,
Whipped up by westerly air.

The fresh song of a fen skylark
Over the flat fields streams
To the lorry park
Full of lorry schemes.

Nothing human moves.
The lark and the breeze continue
While the new wheat grows
And the new day's dew

Slides into the widening world
And a comfortable man may
Climb into a cab, unfurl
A lorry-load of potatoes. Away

The diesel engine racks;
The juggernaut gathers speed
And rolls up the slope. Soundtracks
In the yard recede.

Crumbling Shed

At the corner of the car park a token shed remains;
A monumental misfit, its interior contains
Approximately eight corroding staging blocks.

In days when swish theatricals in the hall were all the rage
Much entertaining acting lit that naive, post-war age
With pantomimes performed with hope like Goldilocks.

Red Riding Hood, Aladdin, these were very popular:
Fantastic tales from countries so immeasurably far.
Strange keys were found to turn the battered old shed's locks.

Pulled back, the doors gave up their secrets, spiders disappeared
And cats rebounded, sprinted off and light admitted speared
The stacked array of coffin shapes. Outside the flocks

Of rooks that crouched on perches bare were muffled, sprouting
eyes
That focused on the shed where plywood forms of even size
Were tugged into the morning bright like precious rocks.

The shed was then shut and secured with indolent delight,
Abandoned, not now needed, once more put out of sight;
Wildlife slouched inside to live - without eight stage blocks.

Pub Wall With Agricultural Connections

This Tardis room where many stand
Or sit with pint of beer in hand,
Its walls a place of history
Of hereabouts, each century,
And even now, as times are strained,
The tales once told are still retained
When men were men behind the plough,
When women swept and cooked, somehow
Raised families and hand-washed clothes,
Mended them, maintained a pose
Of competence and then expired.
State education slow conspired
To raise the stakes and then two wars
Allowed ploughmen still work outdoors,
Walk up and down the crops of beet
Till tractors finally brought defeat;
Sprays, combine harvesters and then
No work left for these gangs of men.
Now few take part in farming games:
Most daily drive to City trains.
And yet the pub is still alight,
Splays echoed laughter every night.

Old Lorry Body

Set down by a ditch to aid conservation
Is a store place for tools in a strange aggregation
Of clippers and mowers and barrows and shears
Protected from pilferers for all these years;
Only allowed out when what was intended
Was using the mower or it had to be mended
Or the ditch was quite clogged up by terrible weed,
The trees needed pruning, the thistles in seed,
Mud pathways demanded bark chippings and then
More barrows of chippings and more and just then
The rain turned to snow and the cart shed caved in
With a creak and a crack and a terrible din.
In the summer the cattle terrorised passers-by,
A woodpecker was spotted low down in the sky,
A fen-blow began after weeks of a drought
Making sheep queasily totter about.
Young and old conservationists threatened to quit,
Lock the door of the lorry-shed, abandon it.
But all of a sudden the clouds went away,
Leaving sunshine and laughter to fill up the day,
So out came the mower, the sickle, the rake;
Work went on till sunset way down by the lake.
How hard they all toiled , everybody agreed,
Hurrah, conservationists - What a fine breed!

Missing Wall

What was it once, joined up closely
To the cottage that remains?
Few hints survive; some minor stains,
No signs of torture and no chains.

Below, in the slow incoming tide
Of stinging nettles, grass, docks,
No gallows stand, no ancient stocks
Nor thumbscrews to rewind the clocks.

I feel I must hold the evidence,
Point a finger over its surface,
Know what lies before its face;
Find out if it hides some disgrace.

Stand back – A lorry passes me by,
Shuffling down the lane to the fen.
The wall starts history again,
Black-tarred shiplap. Now and then

Some hint of movement, speaking inside
The wooden shed from years long gone,
Things moved about, jobs left undone
Then silence. The past had begun

To settle its feathers, look around
Here. Spreading out, history plays
On stage. Casts spiral on parade,
The wall peels, the memory fades.

Tall Manor Wall

It's tall, so very, very, very tall,
Beside the Manor House, the Manor's wall.
Consider, as you slouch by, deep in thought,
Was ever, over there, a giraffe brought
From far away by boat and special lorry?
If this is so, I am so very sorry;
No animal thus kept can keep in touch
Sufficient for life's meaning to be much.
A wall as tall as that is a constriction,
Denying sense, a contradiction.
Why, unseen beings, passing by that way,
Might thus address each other, say,
'And how are you?' and, 'How the cost of eggs
Has rocketed! The trouble with my legs
Is worse, not better. Best be getting on
Before the bus to Ely Market's gone.'
I'm not surprised that no-one knows about
Its solitude. To me there is no doubt
The wall made the giraffe feel ill at ease
Indeed, brought forth some dire giraffe disease;
A sudden weakening in its life thus meant
It died. The wall might be its monument.

House Corner

My ancestor, Howard, built this house
With his own hands.
He was a practical man,
Short, popular with the neighbours,
Laugh a firework,
Arms iron levers,
Always in trouble
With the law.

Wanted it to be his one, true memorial
For his young wife
Who had loved him all the days,
Never spoke a word against him,
Smile of an angel,
Heart of a lion,
Dreaming of a bounty
In a son.

Thought they were round the corner,
The child soon due;
Piteous her labour pains,
Cries the size of thunder up above.
Death took the baby,
Took away his lass
So he drove west of Coveney
On his own.

Left the sad house behind him;
No coming back.
Cancelled his connections;
Slept beside the Hundred Foot.
Reels of stars remaining,
No secure perspective,
Memories a kaleidoscope
Of endless curves.

Strange Farm Shed

I walked; the springtime light took my self away
Through mesmerising gnats gasping the air;
Both eyes became transfigured by a share
Of outspread being as I felt the length of road
Wake up my feet. I strode
Much further than I meant, that lovely day.

No houses; birds called out, hid and broke away;
Hedges of hawthorn looked at me in pride,
So full of growth. High up on either side
Were earthy verges, grassed and shaded green,
Still very short. I'd seen
An old farm shed kneel down as if to pray.

Stop walking; creepers don't care to fall away,
Keep wrapping tightly walls of wood and stone.
And bladed brambles, raucous, overgrown,
Trying to stifle any rising cry
From what's inside. Go by,
Don't wait to hear interior voices say,

'I can see your look - You mustn't walk away!
My time had gone but come to this, my wall;
Come closer, place both hands upon my small
Glass pane. Reach up and look deep through its heart
Which holds the future part
Of our connection that should grow today.'

These words; I rolled them up, threw them far away
Over the hedge, the field, the distant hill.
Like fireworks they exploded time until
I could no longer move: my wrists were tied.
What was it, there inside,
I wondered? Was my reluctance delay?

I woke; a mist thicker than the dreariest day
Took stranglehold and dragged me round about,
Hands on my eyes, my ears; I tried to shout
But senselessness, despotic, took my head;
Soon my whole self was dead.
No answer then and I can't walk away.

Strange Clunch

So oddly out of place and yet
The clunch wall claims its space;

Edged by red bricks,
Smoothed by the winds
Of underwater regions.
Willowy sea creatures watched
It building.
Centuries slid by

Slow tidal ebbs and flows
So slowly it grows.

 In late times,
Quarried and carted by lorry to be used,
Stone by stone
Locked into place,
A wall.

So oddly in its place they let
The fossil pile maintain that space, that wall.

Once, I remember, it bordered a shop
Selling sweets,
Popular with children
Wandering in with pennies;
Uncertain choices, liquorice in sherbet,
Gob stoppers, sweet cigarettes,
Aniseed balls, Mars
Bars,
All, all slightly dated
Though not as old
As clunch.

Cart Shed

Cart shed,
Pretty;
Well, it's meant to be
A parcel-place for rusting iron
Saved from extinction, almost.
Now we only stilly stare,
Its trundled insides like old horses in old age,
A challenge to watch, to pity, glorify,
The gods of long-gone earthy agricultural idylls;
Blocked almost out but kept alive
In black and white pictures
Taken on Box Brownies.

Next rests an airy, open-fronted part,
Umbrella roof, a roundabout information pack
Concerning wild woodland, flowers,
Birds' plumage, insects.

A blink away there is
A most comforting seat. Sit there and you
Will sink into today; the breeze, some cloud,
Rough grass beneath your feet, a view all round
The patch, the light relief
That is always free for all.

Look back – The cart shed glances out
From indistinct shadow, knows you're drowned
But golden.

Brick Bus Stop Wall

Keep looking for the coming of the minibus today,
Rooting through the village then on to Market Street,
Looking down Main Street,
Wider by the School where a dozen mothers meet
And chat to other mothers, wave goodbye and walk away.

There's one man coming walking in a disconnected way,
Rapidly, with paper to read when he gets home,
Thinks he is alone;
A second with his thumb on a fancy mobile phone
In agitated gestures; there is much he has to say.

A slatted wooden seat is built to cater for delay,
For weary ones to sit on, count the minutes slide,
Slowly ebb the tide.
Bus doors soon will open up and they climb up inside
And settle for the twenty minutes ride to Mandalay.

The shelter is abandoned now so emptiness will stay,
Frozen for an hour till a second bus can come.
Any use has gone.
The dull rows of its brick design so clearly meant to stun:
This neglected waiting place is little used today.

Bishop's Palace

Masada, in Israel, is a high mountain place
Where King Herod decided to use up some space
To the north, on the hillside, away from the sun
So his builders got building, worked hard, everyone,
For if anyone slouched, hoping times might be slow,
King Herod would scowl and the man's head would go.

In no time the incredible palace was there
On that wonderful hanging rock, up in the air,
So cool in the summer, away from the toil
Of Jerusalem politics, tensions and spoil;
A place to look forward to, sitting it out
In soft breezes, nice cocktails, just lazing about.

'So what', you may wonder, 'has all this to do
With that palace in Downham? Please give us a clue!'
Well, it's not the dimensions, nor temperature
Of our long days of summer, of that I am sure.
No, the only connection's the northerly clue
That places their faces alike for the view.

As Herod snoozed moodily, gently perspired,
The bishops of Ely much later conspired
To sneak off to Downham, three miles down the track,
To their summer residence, elegant shack,
Abandoning choirboys and canons and those
Theological conundrums that tickled the nose.

Though the Hurst Road was muddy to their summer home
And the flies buzzed continuously, making them groan,
The thought of relaxing, a bit out of sight,
Was wonderful magic, filled hearts with delight
As, close by the golf course near Ely they passed
Bright Downham's slight hilltop came closer at last.

So why is it nowadays no bishops come
To stay here, to dream here, perhaps have some fun?
Can it be that now Eurostar beckons them go
Into European cities, perhaps Tokyo,
Or down south to Africa, westwards the States
Go surfing off Zanzibar, Tunisian dates?

Every person in Downham, confused, set apart
From bishops in summers, holds this to the heart –
They don't need to worry, they don't need to make
Attentive allusions nor yet make a cake
But can get on with gossiping, watching 'The News',
Clean the windows, read papers, whatever they choose!

Cemetery Wall

A wall holds this curious place. All is still,
The confusion of living loss;
Inhabitants claim this side of the slight hill
Constrained by a closed roof of grass and moss.

Wild primroses scatter their kindred around
With pale-paint petals that spread
The morning sun's warmth, the touch of the wild ground
In the token land of the sober dead.

Beating wild birds lift up into the air,
Fleck interim spaces with cries
Rebounding in ripples, filling everywhere
With music that muffles underground sighs,

Teases visitors of every kind
Who contemplate the many gone
And who come here in hopelessness, maybe to find
Slight, insecure memories stutteringly come.

Contents

Printed in Great Britain
by Amazon

22243695R00066